Dust Bunnies
in the
Basket

*Finding God
in Lent & Easter*

Tim Schenck

ISBN 978-0-88028-403-5

Printed in USA

Forward Movement
www.forwardmovement.org

Dedication

To my sons Benedict and Zachary,
from a father who couldn't be prouder.

Table of Contents

Acknowledgments

This book seemed like a natural companion to *Dog in the Manger: Finding God in Christmas Chaos.* Frankly, I didn't want "Dog" to be lonely so I figured a Lent/Easter volume made sense. Fortunately Scott Gunn, Richelle Thompson, and the good folks at Forward Movement agreed.

As some of you know, I have a thing about Lent. In 2010 I created Lent Madness with the goal of getting people to reimagine the season. Lent Madness is a unique Lenten devotion, a fun and engaging way for people to learn about the saints. Lent shouldn't be grim and depressing. After all, what could be more joyful than a season specifically set aside to grow closer to Jesus? So I'm glad to share this journey from Lent to Easter with all of you.

In the acknowledgments section for the last book, I referred to my wife, Bryna, as "beautiful and talented." She never ceases to remind me of this, but it leaves me with a quandary—how do you top *that*?

I guess I'll need to thank my smart and stunning wife this time. Phew!

My boys Benedict and Zachary are never particularly impressed when one of my books arrives. It might be because they usually appear in some of the essays, and, well, they're teenagers. Thanks, boys, for keeping me grounded. And, yes, I realize I know next to nothing.

I would be remiss if I didn't thank my writing partner: coffee. Thanks for the inspiration. And thanks to Bob and the crew at Redeye Roasters for always keeping me well caffeinated.

Finally, I'm grateful to my parishioners at the Episcopal Parish of St. John the Evangelist in Hingham, Massachusetts. It continues to be a privilege to serve among you as your rector.

Introduction

The first Sunday in Lent is always awkward since I never quite know how to greet people. I can't really say "Happy Lent," and "Merry Lent" certainly doesn't work. Nothing quite rolls off the tongue because I'm not always sure how to approach this season of spiritual preparation.

Lent is a very personal time of reflection and introspection as we examine our lives and our relationship with God, coming face-to-face with our own sinfulness and mortality. Lent is most fully experienced within the context of a worshiping community—we don't enter into the season in isolation.

Still, this doesn't answer our question of what to say to people at coffee hour. Fortunately, the Ash Wednesday liturgy gives us a clue. We are invited on behalf of the Church to the observance of a holy Lent. Not a successful or productive or guilt-ridden or dour or twig-eating Lent, but a holy Lent.

So, maybe that's our answer. We can bid one another a holy Lent. This makes a lot more sense than wishing one another a happy Lent or even a gloomy Lent. This season of Lent is often misunderstood, and our confusion about how to greet one another at its start reflects the fact that we don't always know how to approach it. Lent is not meant to be the Church's season of depression. It's not a time to walk around with sad faces, doing our best to look miserable. Sometimes we equate holiness with misery: the more miserable we are, the more holy we must be. But that's not fair to the concept of holiness.

To be holy means to be set apart in a special way. A holy Lent is a joyful Lent because it draws us closer to the heart of God. It sets us apart, keeping us focused on the spiritual priorities of our lives and our single most important relationship—our relationship with God. It's not a time to be overly grim but an opportunity to be drawn into ever-deepening relationship with the risen Christ. Yes, there may be painful moments in this. Introspection is never easy. But in our inadequacy and weakness, the loving grace of God shines ever more brightly.

So in this light, I bid you a holy Lent. I hope this book serves as a companion on your spiritual

journey. At the end of each chapter, I've provided some questions to use for personal reflection or group study. I pray that the book and reflections help draw you ever closer to the God of compassion and mercy as we move through the wilderness into resurrection glory.

— **Tim Schenck**

LENT

Dust Bunnies

I don't like dust, and I especially don't like dust bunnies. You know those mysterious furry things that lurk behind your bedroom door, or in your closet, or under your bed. Who knows how they got there? Who wants to know how they got there? But they're there, and I don't like them, especially when they move around. You've probably seen them do this: you open a door, look behind it, and the dust bunny catches just enough air that it seems to start hopping away.

Cleanliness may or may not be next to godliness but dust bunnies show up whether or not we're compulsive dusters. Even Mr. Clean himself occasionally sees dust bunnies in his pantry closet—and his clean-shaven, earring-wearing self is horrified.

So, it's not the most comforting thought in the world on Ash Wednesday when we receive the sign of the cross on our foreheads with the words, "Remember that you are dust and to dust you shall return."

Fortunately, this doesn't turn us into walking, talking dust bunnies. God's not going to sweep us away with a giant feather duster. But the words of the Ash Wednesday service remind us that there is something greater out there, greater than what we can see with the naked eye, greater than our hopes, fears, and dreams. And that something is God. It's not that we're as insignificant, useless, and annoying as dust bunnies; it's just that the world doesn't revolve around dust, and it doesn't revolve around us. God is the center of all life and creation, which doesn't mean we're useless; we're just not in control.

Think about dust for a moment. There are two ways to create it, through inactivity and activity. If you go downstairs into the part of the basement that rarely gets used, the part where you store old boxes full of books or that pair of cross-country skis you've long since outgrown, you encounter dust. Run your finger along those skis and you get a tangible reminder that they haven't been used in ages. Your finger is suddenly covered with dust, and you might even sneeze once or twice.

Then there's the other way dust is created, through activity. That's how those dust bunnies in your bedroom came to be. Through the everyday activity of life, you create dust. It comes in on your shoes or your clothes, or on the kids' backpacks. If we're not kicking up some dust, we're not really living.

Jesus encourages us to kick up some dust every now and then, to roll up our sleeves and get involved with the world and the people around us. We might get dirty every once in a while, but that's okay. Through our relationship with Jesus we are cleansed, renewed, and dusted off time and time again.

All of this is why I like to hold a children's Ash Wednesday service every year. Not many churches do this because there's a natural inclination to shield our kids from concepts like mortality and human sin. And the idea of dumping ashes on the heads of young children and telling them they'll eventually die gives some clergy the willies. But ignoring an important and integral part of life isn't the answer. You certainly don't have to spook children to make the point—though I do know a woman who went to Catholic school and for years was convinced that the ashes themselves came from the bones of dead nuns.

I simply like to make age-appropriate connections for children that hopefully lead to further questions. On Shrove Tuesday (aka Mardi Gras), we burn the palms from the previous Palm Sunday. At the next day's Ash Wednesday service, I invite the children to sit with me as I use a mortar and pestle to create the ashes. As I grind the burnt palms and strain out the larger pieces, I talk about life, death, and resurrection. Then I administer the ashes on their foreheads. Rather than removing the mystery, I find this process draws them deeper into the story and makes the entrance into the season of Lent that much more tangible.

Of course, one year I had just imposed ashes at the children's service with the words "Remember that you are dust and to dust you shall return," when a little girl looked up and asked, "Pixie dust?" Sure. Why not?

Sinful Delight

"Sinful Delight." I saw this listed on a dessert menu recently, just under the crème brûlée. It was a concoction containing chocolate mousse, homemade whipped cream, and a few caramel swirls. In other words, not something you'd want to confront if you'd given up chocolate for Lent. But it got me thinking about how little we talk about sin these days. Sure, we'll label a few items on the dessert tray "sinful," but when it comes to confronting true sinfulness—that which separates us from God—we've already paid the check and started for home.

Sin is not a topic most of us care to discuss, yet if we fully and authentically enter into the season of Lent, we cannot avoid the subject of sin. Indeed in the Collect for Ash Wednesday, we pray that God may "create and make in us new and contrite hearts, that we, worthily lamenting our sins and acknowledging our wretchedness, may obtain of you, the God of all mercy, perfect remission and forgiveness" (*The Book of Common Prayer*, p. 264).

Acknowledging our wretchedness doesn't sound like much fun, but it does emphasize the severity and depth of the issue. We are all sinners; it is part of who we are as human beings. To deny or minimize this fact is to deny or minimize God's capacity for mercy and forgiveness. We can't reflect on our sinfulness without also reflecting on God's loving providence, because even when we separate ourselves from God, God still desires us. Even when we fail to honor those in our midst, God still seeks healing, and even when we feel unlovable, God still loves us.

But sin is difficult to discuss. If we dwell too much on it, we negate the joy of life lived in the Spirit.

And if we take it too lightly, we risk a cheapened, rudderless faith. As in most things, striking the proper balance is key.

As Luther said, 'Sin boldly!'

Sin needs to be acknowledged and confessed but always within the context of God's grace. Our job as faithful Christians is to come before God, not just saying the words of the confession on Sunday mornings but repenting in our hearts and showing forth that repentance through amendment of life. We say in the Rite I absolution, "Almighty God, our heavenly Father, who of his great mercy hath promised forgiveness of sins to all those who with hearty repentance and true faith turn unto him, have mercy upon you, pardon and deliver you from all your sins, confirm and strengthen you in all goodness, and bring you to everlasting life, through Jesus Christ our Lord" (*The Book of Common Prayer*, p. 332). The point of reflecting on our sins is that we grow and change, that we explore and deepen the salvific relationship with Jesus that is so graciously extended to each one of us.

So, unless you have given up chocolate for Lent, go ahead and order that "Sinful Delight." It may be a guilty pleasure, but it's certainly not sinful. If sin is that which separates us from God, dessert doesn't qualify. No matter how much it may separate us from our previous pants size.

Tuning Peg

When I was a kid, I sometimes tagged along with my father to symphony orchestra rehearsals. He was a conductor with the Baltimore Symphony Orchestra in the 1970s. When a babysitter got sick or my mother was working, I'd accompany him to the old Lyric Theater in downtown Baltimore. When I wasn't hanging out in the dressing room with the poker-playing horn players or wandering around backstage among the huge double bass cases and assorted timpani drums, I'd be out exploring the red velvet-lined boxes in the balcony. Looking back, these were pretty special moments, memories I particularly cherish since my father died of cancer at fifty-two.

You could say that one of the soundtracks of my childhood was the tuning of the orchestra. If you've ever been to a classical music concert, you know that they all start with the same ritual tuning. After a nod from the concertmaster, the principal oboe player gives them an A and then the rest of the orchestra tunes their instruments off of the note of the oboe, which, of all the instruments, provides the truest pitch. It just took a few moments, but they always tuned up at the beginning of the rehearsal and then periodically throughout if my father heard something that didn't sound quite right.

The spiritual life is a bit like an orchestra in this regard. Over time, instruments naturally get out of tune if left alone. Strings in particular are very sensitive to cold or humidity. A violin string might stretch out, causing it to go flat. Or it might constrict, causing it to go sharp. A violinist must do a bit of fine-tuning with the pegs to get the instrument back in playing condition.

In a sense, the season of Lent is the church's tuning peg. Because our priorities can become slightly off-key, Lent brings us back into tune, allowing and encouraging us to live again in harmony with God. It's easy to let our spiritual lives get away from us. We get busy; we get self-absorbed; we get bogged down by endless activity. We let the minutiae of life drive our priorities, and suddenly we find ourselves out of tune with the Spirit. It might be so subtle that we hardly notice that our spiritual life has gone a bit flat, or it might be strident, atonal disharmony. Either way,

Lent holds the potential to bring our spiritual lives back into tune. It encourages self-reflection and a return to the basics of our faith.

Lent forces us to reconsider the priorities of our lives. It demands we face the questions about what is truly important. There's a natural sifting of the superfluous and nonessential pieces of our lives that brings us back to the brass tacks of the human experience. The basics of family and friends, shelter, food, and helping others in need are what remain. And at the heart of these is our relationship with the living God, the God who creates, redeems, and sanctifies us, the God who joins us on the journey of life and faith, whatever trials and tribulations we meet along the way.

Throughout Lent, I encourage you to allow your spiritual tuning peg to be turned, if even just slightly. It requires obedience to the ultimate conductor of our lives yet results in ever-increasing peace, joy, love, and harmony.

Reflection & Discussion

1 What has been your experience with the Ash Wednesday liturgy over the years? How does reflecting on the imposition of ashes and the phrase "Remember that you are dust and to dust you shall return" impact your spiritual life? Do you remember attending this service as a child? If so, how has your understanding of receiving ashes evolved?

2 Have you ever felt your spiritual life has become slightly off-key? What are the signs or feelings you've experienced that led you to believe this to be true? What methods have you used or are you using to "tune up" your relationship with God?

3 How do you define sin? Do you believe the ubiquitous list of seven deadly sins—wrath, greed, sloth, pride, lust, envy, and gluttony—is complete? How does the recognition of your own sinfulness impact the way you live your life?

LENT DEUX

Death by Chocolate

I always give up chocolate for Lent. I can't claim super-human willpower or an unnaturally pious existence. The truth is I don't like chocolate. I'm not allergic to it; it doesn't make me break out in hives. I just don't like it. And in the eyes of most red-blooded Americans, this makes me suspect. When I politely decline an after-dinner mint or a mid-day Hershey bar, people give me strange looks and some literally back away in horror as if they've encountered a leper.

But this doesn't stop me from dramatically turning down offers of fudge during the Church's season of penitence. Ah, the virtue of it all! Just don't ask me to give up Fritos.

Giving up chocolate, of course, is the Lenten discipline's equivalent of a poster child. Who hasn't tried to give up chocolate for Lent? And who hasn't failed? But this Lenten cliché does draw us into a deeper point about our spiritual lives. Lenten

disciplines are great, but they must be made in the context of the God of all grace. God still loves us even when we sneak a chocolate chip cookie. God still loves us when we fall short in our Lenten disciplines and in our lives. Perhaps this divine forgiveness is the heart of the Christian faith, the reason we bother at all with Lenten disciplines. Failing to give up our guilty pleasures shouldn't lead to guilt—surely that's not the point of keeping a holy Lent.

Each year, the great Lenten debate centers upon whether to give something up or take something on. The general consensus is that giving something up is "old school" while taking something on is more devotional in nature. I don't believe these two are mutually exclusive. Why not give up red meat and say Morning Prayer each day?

Giving up something for Lent can be a wonderful spiritual discipline. Like fasting, it is an act of self-denial, but even more than this, it can set our hearts on God. The emptiness can be a physical reminder that our needs are only satisfied through faith in Jesus Christ. The Ash Wednesday invitation to observe a holy Lent calls us to do so "by self-examination and repentance; by prayer, fasting and self-denial; and by reading and meditating on God's holy Word" (*The Book of Common Prayer,* p. 265). In other words, a holy Lent calls for a balanced blend of giving up and taking on.

Yet even giving up and taking on during Lent offers its own challenges—especially if you view Lenten disciplines as merely sacred versions of New Year's resolutions. Of course there's nothing wrong with New Year's resolutions. Nearly everyone resolves to lose weight, exercise more, or amend their spending habits. Unfortunately, these resolutions rarely have anything to do with our spiritual lives. The purpose of our Lenten disciplines is to strengthen our spiritual lives and ultimately to bring us closer to the heart of Jesus.

As for me, I'll be giving up chocolate again this Lent. Yes, the smell of it makes my stomach turn. And I worry the classic dessert "Death by Chocolate" could actually kill me, so it's not much of a cross to bear. And if you're still not sure about the value of giving something up, consider this: a few years ago I heard about a priest in the Church of England who gave up preaching for Lent. Talk about the potential for a mutually beneficial experience!

Giving it Up

Encouraging kids to give things up for Lent is a losing battle. At least it was in our house when our boys were younger. Ben and Zak were perfectly willing to give up certain things, like math homework or visits to the dentist, but suggest chocolate or their beloved video games and they'd stare at you like you had three heads.

As a good parish priest, I'd talk to the boys about the importance of the season, how Christians connect with Jesus' forty days spent in the wilderness. How Lent is a time of self-denial and repentance, an opportunity to return to the basics of faith while taking stock of life's priorities. Or I'd tell them to think of it as the spiritual equivalent of a spring cleaning. People seek to eradicate the bad habits or apathy that have slowly crept into their lives and replace this with a healthier, God-centered approach to life.

The boys, shockingly, didn't go for all my Lenten philosophizing, and self-denial is tough enough for

adults. Sure, some of us will give up carbs or dessert for Lent, but have we made this sacrifice to renew our relationship with God or because of the health or dietary benefits? Dig deep enough, and we find that many of our Lenten disciplines are really things that will make us better or better-looking people—but do not necessarily bring us closer to God.

This gets at the classic Lenten "reversal"—taking something on rather than giving something up for Lent. This is also a tough sell for kids but nonetheless an important idea. Each Lent we used to get those small cardboard Lenten Mite Boxes at our parish. The kids took them home and dropped some coins into them each week. At the end of Lent, they were shipped off to the charity that the parish was supporting that year.

One Lent I remember Zak simply couldn't get his young mind around the fact that he was being asked to give his money away. Even thinking about putting money into the box would reduce him to tears. Talk about your sacrificial giving! Bryna and I gave him some simple tasks to perform around the house so he could earn some money with the caveat that he'd put a small portion into the box. He'd nod his head, eagerly wipe the kitchen floor with a few paper towels, and then start wailing when it came time to pay the piper. I got so fed up with this whole Lenten lesson that I eventually gave him some of my money to put into the box just so he could have something to turn in, which completely defeated the purpose.

I was not going to force the boys to take up a Lenten discipline. I couldn't see making them fast on Fridays for instance, unless I wanted a call from child protective services. Nor could I see compelling them to engage in contemplative prayer for half an hour each day. Words like force and compel didn't seem in keeping with the spiritual life. But I did want to model spiritual behavior and to show them that Lent is a holy time, an opportunity to grow closer to God. That is why our tradition became reading a Bible story together at bedtime during the evenings of Lent. At times they loved the ritual of it and sometimes they whined about it, but I could always find some violent battle in the Old Testament to keep them interested.

God's Country

Isaw the most amazing sight while in southern California a few years ago. After flying out for a midweek conference in San Diego, I stayed through the weekend to guest preach at a friend's church in Palm Desert. Having never been out that way, I was mesmerized by the two-and-a-half-hour drive into the desert. The waterfront quickly gave way to rolling green hills, which morphed into giant rock-covered mountains full of cacti and, I was told, rattlesnakes. The topography was near Biblical—stunningly wild and beautiful.

I even had a roadrunner pointed out to me as it scampered across the landscape. For someone who had only seen one on Saturday morning cartoons, this was impressive. Sure, we have coyotes in Massachusetts but definitely not road-runners.

None of this is what truly captured my imagination or made me do a triple take. That moment came just as we neared the peak of the highest mountain. A

young couple had pulled to the side of the road, and they were standing just slightly away from their car. At first I thought maybe they had engine trouble and we slowed down. Then in an instant it became clear what they were doing: the young man was taking a picture of a tiny patch of snow.

Imagine! Someone who had probably grown up in the desert wanting to record a rare remnant of cold weather. My first thought was "Picture? Get me a shovel!" It was February, after all, and I had just escaped the New England winter for a brief respite.

But then I started reflecting on the power of different perspectives. We were both mesmerized by what we saw that day—we just came at it from diametrically opposed angles. As I thought about it, snow in the desert is an incredible sight. And if he thought about it, I'm sure he would recognize that the ancient rock formation upon which this small amount of snow lay was also extraordinary. We could have mocked one another for our respective parochialism—that's what people usually do when confronted with different perspectives. Yet it's the diversity of viewpoints that enriches us and gets at the fullness of an elusive truth.

Driving through the desert during Lent made me think about the forty days and forty nights that Jesus spent in the wilderness before starting his public ministry. This season mirrors Jesus' time in the desert and helps Christians walk the way of the cross that leads to Easter joy.

Each one of us takes a different spiritual path. There's no one-size-fits-all when it comes to faith. Some of us might encounter two-foot snow drifts; others 120-degree desert heat. Yet as our Lenten journeys bring us closer to God, we recognize that while we don't have all the answers, we do have unique experiences worth sharing.

Leave It!

O ne of the first commands I learned at dog obedience school was "Leave it!" Actually our rescued yellow lab/husky, Delilah, was supposedly the student, but you know how these things work. To learn this command I put Delilah in the down position and covered a treat with one hand. Then I slowly took my hand away to reveal the treat and said, "Leave it!" If Delilah started to go for the treat, I quickly placed my hand back over it and started the process again. Once she was able to leave it, she got the treat.

After awhile I was able to put the treat in front of her, say "leave it," and she just stared at it with puppy dog eyes until I let her have it.

This command isn't taught to dogs as a form of psychological torture; the point is to teach them to listen to their owner when they're supposed to leave something alone. Like a shoe or a plant or that entire bowl of wonton soup Delilah once helped herself to as I turned my back for a split second. Yet, as I worked with Delilah on this obedience training, it also felt like an exercise in resisting temptation.

This, of course, is a big theme during Lent. Jesus encounters the devil in the wilderness and is tempted to give into cravings of hunger, the allure of wealth, and the thirst for power. Instead of saying "Man does not live by bread alone," Jesus could have turned a stone into a bagel or a loaf of pumpernickel or even a doughnut. But he doesn't, and the preparation for his public ministry continues.

Jesus may well have had one of those cartoon moments with the angel on one shoulder and a devil on the other shoulder. "Don't do it. Remain faithful" says the one. "Go ahead and turn that stone into a dinner roll. It's not a big deal," says the other. And while it must have been tempting, Jesus resists and stays true to the work he has been given to do. Jesus is tempted as we are yet does not sin and refuses to give into temptation. The fact that Jesus experiences temptation at all shows his ability to identify and empathize with our own challenges.

We've all been tempted in various ways by various things. We live in a culture that screams out, "Eat me, drink me, buy me, look at me, listen to me, sleep with me." Temptation abounds. Lay's potato chips used to have a slogan, "No one can eat just one" and that pretty much sums up our culture. "I bet you can't eat just one; I bet you can't live without HDTV; I bet you can't look your best without Botox; I bet you can't be happy without a Coors Light."

People sometimes ask me about the line in the Lord's Prayer, "Lead us not into temptation." Why, they wonder, would God lead anyone into temptation in the first place? It's a good question. There may be an element of testing involved for all of us—the Old Testament image of being thrust into the refiner's fire to take away our impurities comes to mind. But I also point to the modern version of the Lord's Prayer that many scholars believe is closer to the ancient Greek. The line doesn't speak about being led into temptation but instead reads, "Save us from the time of trial." We've all certainly experienced times of trial in our lives, times of anguish, grief, pain, or depression. And there is nothing rawer than praying for God to save us. It's a cry of both desperation and hope. Whatever we call it, temptation is a very real and powerful force.

I always thought I should try to teach the "Leave it" command to the boys. To teach them a lesson about temptation, I could put a hunk of double fudge brownie in the middle of the table and tell them to "Leave it." Or dangle two brand new iPhones in front of their faces and command them to "Leave it." I have a feeling I'd get injured.

Reflection & Discussion

1 Reflect on some Lenten disciplines in which you've engaged. Have they been successful? Fruitful? Why or why not? What are you considering giving up and/or taking on this year? In what other ways will you seek to keep a holy Lent?

2 How has your approach to Lent evolved over the years? Do you embrace it as a joyful season of spiritual renewal or does it feel like a depressing season of sack cloth and twig eating? In what ways does your church mark the season—visually, musically, programmatically, and liturgically?

3 Read the story of Jesus' temptation in the wilderness in Matthew 4. In what ways can you relate to his experience of being in the wilderness? What are the powerful temptations that most affect you? What strategies have been helpful over the years in resisting temptation?

HOLY WEEK

Palm Sunday Rewrite

Listening to the story of Christ's Passion on Palm Sunday always frustrates me. Amid the familiar hymns, the red vestments, and leafy palms, the ending never changes. At various points, I want to jump into the story and shake some sense into the characters or yell "cut!" and give the Passion readers a new script. Every year I wait for a different conclusion: maybe Jesus makes a dramatic escape, or his divinity is recognized before the crucifixion, or he invokes God to take him down from the cross. But the ending is always the same: Jesus is left hanging on the cross to die, and we're left helplessly and hopelessly watching from the sidelines.

I find some places in the Passion narrative especially frustrating. I'll bet I'm not alone.

■ THE GARDEN OF GETHSEMANE. I want to yell at the three disciples, "Stay awake! What's wrong with you? I don't care how tired you are. Rest some other time! Or drink a can of Red Bull." Of course Peter, James, and John are human, and they're weak. They don't know what's about to take place. We do.

■ THE ARREST OF JESUS. The disciples start to fight with the chief priests and the crowd. Jesus stops them and tells them to put their swords away, and all I can think is, "Jesus, please call on those twelve legions of angels you say God would provide if only you asked. You could subdue this mob and get away. Do it!" Like the disciples, our first instinct is anger. We too want to put up a fight because we know Jesus is falsely accused. But Jesus knows that the unveiling of God's plan doesn't always match our own wants and desires.

■ THE ENCOUNTER WITH THE HIGH PRIEST. Jesus stands silent before his accusers. He is mocked, spit upon, and beaten. "OK, Jesus. You didn't run away when you had the chance, but speak for God's sake! Tell them who you really are. Show them who you really are. Do a sign, perform a miracle. Maybe then they'll realize they've made a terrible mistake and let you go." We know who Jesus is, but his accusers do not. Jesus knows what must be done to fulfill the scriptures and redeem humanity. No one else can know what the Son of God knows.

■ **PILATE'S OFFER TO RELEASE JESUS OR BARABBAS.** The crowd wants blood. More specifically, they want Jesus' blood. I want to shout: "Release Jesus! He's innocent. Come to your senses and let him go. You have the power to set God's son free." But the choice is made, Barabbas walks away, and another opportunity to change the story is lost.

■ **JESUS ON THE CROSS.** The crowd mockingly shouts, "If you are the Son of God, come down from the cross." Jesus cries out to God but remains nailed to the wood. I plead: "Jesus, come down, please. Wouldn't this be a great chance to show everyone who you really are? Come down off that cross and live." Why doesn't Jesus save himself? Is it possible that he couldn't? Doubt begins to creep in.

My notion of a proper ending never transpires. Jesus Christ, my Lord and yours, is mocked, derided, and crucified. We know how the story goes. It barrels ahead in all its gruesome familiarity, and as frustrating as it is, we can't do anything to change it. The spirit will be willing, but the flesh will be weak.

Peter will deny Christ three times, Barabbas will be released, Pilate will wash his hands, and Jesus will be crucified.

The script can't be sent back for a rewrite, and no one knows this better than Jesus himself. As the drama unfolds, he prays, "Yet, not what I want, but what you want" (Mark 14:36). This is exactly how we must approach the Passion narrative. Christ offers himself to God for us, and we must accept this offer. We may not understand exactly why Christ has to die in order for humanity to be redeemed, but we must allow God's purposes to be fulfilled whether or not we fully comprehend or agree with what takes place.

In our own lives we often make judgments about why certain things happen to us without fully knowing the breadth of God's plan for us. This is why the beginning of Holy Week offers no better starting point than to pray with Jesus, "Yet, not what I want, but what you want."

Dirty Feet

No one likes dirty feet. More to the point, no one likes someone else's dirty feet. Yet that's a major theme on the Thursday before Easter. Whether it's called Maundy Thursday or Holy Thursday, foot washing is often an integral part of the Holy Week experience.

The practice of foot washing comes out of the story of the Last Supper. Presumably the disciples who gathered with Jesus in the Upper Room didn't like dirty feet either. Even in a culture where it wasn't unusual for another person to wash your feet, this certainly wasn't high on anyone's priority list that night. Jesus' silent movement toward the disciples with a towel, basin, and water pitcher must have drawn some strange looks. What was going on here? The only people who washed feet were the lowest of the lowest classes—not the friend they knew to be the anointed one of God, the Messiah, Jesus the Christ. But there he was, approaching them with towel in hand.

I served at a parish in New York where people didn't just pour water over one another's feet and dry them with a towel. They actually scrubbed one another's feet to the point that the organist had to vamp for fifteen extra minutes because the whole process took so long. At the time I remember thinking, "Okay, enough with the feet; I have a Good Friday sermon to write." But there was something so caring and profoundly moving about this experience that I set aside my snarky thoughts.

I remember the first time I had my feet washed at a Maundy Thursday service. I was in my mid-twenties, but I'd been avoiding it for years. I wanted to have my feet washed, at least in theory. I wanted to experience what the disciples felt that night in the Upper Room. I wanted to be drawn closer to Jesus through the experience, but my discomfort kept me from it.

Each year I'd get closer, but then I'd shy away at the last moment.

I had all sorts of good excuses: It somehow didn't seem church-like. I couldn't imagine taking my shoes off in church. What if I had a hole in my sock? What if my feet smelled? What if they were sweaty or cold? Maybe this command to love one another as Christ loved us, with its visible expression through foot washing, wasn't a literal commandment, maybe it was only meant for the more demonstrative Christians. Couldn't I experience this spiritually rather than physically? It's so public. Maybe it's just not meant for the shy or the introverted or the self-conscious. I don't remember doing this when I was a kid. What about all the people who don't even come to church on Maundy Thursday? At least I'm here.

One year I ran out of excuses. Slowly, against my better judgment, I removed my shoes. Then my socks. I found myself walking toward the foot washing station. As I moved down the main aisle, the stone slabs cooled my feet in an eerie way, and somehow I felt closer to that church and to Christ than I ever had. I learned that our deepest points of relationship with Jesus take us out of our comfort zones.

Having your feet washed is not comfortable. But then, the cross is not comfortable. Christ washes the disciples' feet, not to keep them guessing about his motives but to show them that accepting love can be uncomfortable. Christ calls us to him and loves us always. Even if our feet are dirty.

Happy Birthday

Do you get embarrassed when people sing "Happy Birthday" to you? For me, it is one of the most awkward moments of the year. I know it's coming: all of a sudden several people disappear into the kitchen, there's a slight hush in the air, and out they come parading the birthday cake toward me. And then the singing starts. The familiar tune seems to take an eternity, and there's nothing I can do except sit there with a goofy smile on my face because, of course, I can't sing "Happy Birthday" to myself.

Don't get me wrong. I appreciate the effort, and I love the gathering of family and friends. And I don't mind the presents. It's just that enduring the required serenade while all those people stare makes me a bit uncomfortable. Yet, when I'm celebrating someone else's birthday, I'm the first to belt out "Happy Birthday," usually even adding some harmony to the ending. I like making a fuss over someone else much more than I enjoy being fussed over myself.

Somehow it's more comfortable to celebrate the lives of others than to let others celebrate our lives. And in the context of Maundy Thursday, it's often easier to serve others than to be served. It can be

hard to fully accept someone else's love for us. We ask ourselves, "What's the catch? If someone is going to such great lengths to please me, what can I possibly do in return?" As strange as it may sound, we often resist letting Christ serve us.

Like Peter, we want to say to Jesus, "Lord, you will never wash my feet." We may be embarrassed by the attention or feel that it's beneath the Master to wash our feet. But there's another reason too: our own pride. The real obstacle to letting Christ serve us is that it demands that we put our lives in his hands. It forces us to loosen our grip on the control to which we desperately cling and to allow Christ to be Christ. That's a vulnerable position.

When we allow Christ to be Christ, we're giving him access to our hearts, our thoughts, and our souls. We acknowledge that Christ will take our burdens and our sins and bear them up on his cross. To let Christ be Christ is to find a freedom that is otherwise impossible to know.

Allowing Christ to fully serve us leaves us exposed, just as taking off our shoes in a public place leaves us feeling vulnerable and self-conscious. Participating in a Maundy Thursday foot washing is not comfortable but to walk with Christ, we must take off our shoes, walk barefoot, and put our trust in Christ. The experience allows Christ to be Christ and for him to fully serve us. Like the stripping of the altar that takes place at the end of the Maundy Thursday liturgy, we must be fully exposed to Christ, allowing Jesus to receive us in our nakedness.

A Good Friday

G ood Friday marks the day on which parents deflect the inevitable Holy Week question from children and foist it onto a priest: "If Jesus died on the cross, why is it called Good Friday?" As a service to parents, children, and everyone else who wonders, I offer Father Tim's official response to this classic question. It's called Good Friday because without Jesus' Crucifixion, there would be no Resurrection. So it's good because ultimately we come to Easter and Jesus' rising from the dead. Simple, to the point, and true. If your children want further elaboration, have them email, Facebook, or text me—or however four-year-olds communicate these days.

Even better, have them join me for the Good Friday liturgy. I always find it peculiar that, like Ash Wednesday, more churches don't offer children's services on Good Friday. Kids are drawn to the mystery and ritual and stories of our faith, yet we often exclude them from these experiences. Participating in these liturgies of the church at a young age can have a lasting impact on a person's spiritual life.

No, a four- or six- or even a ten-year-old isn't going to sit reverently and patiently through an hour-long Good Friday service (let alone one of those three-hour deals) but they still need to be brought into the story of the Passion. And this can be done in a variety of ways. A congregation can hold a traditional Good Friday service as well as a children's version of the Stations of the Cross, or even offer a simple telling of the story with props and music. It just takes energy, foresight, and commitment.

I became particularly aware of the need for such a service when I was on sabbatical several years ago. I've always held a brief Good Friday service for the children of the church, but evidently many other congregations do not. At least not the ones I Googled within a twenty-minute drive. I got pretty frustrated trying

to find a Good Friday service appropriate for Ben and Zak. Sure, I could have sat them down and forced them to listen to me read the story of the Crucifixion but hearing whining at the foot of the cross does little for my spiritual life.

In a moment of inspiration, I decided to take them to Maryknoll in Ossining, New York—mere minutes from our house—and walk the outdoor Stations of the Cross. Maryknoll is a Roman Catholic missionary society with an enormous campus. At one time it served as a large training ground for future priests, and they still send missionaries throughout the world. The main building looks like an Asian temple teleported from Beijing to a hill overlooking metropolitan New York. Let's just say the facility stands out.

After lunch I printed out a version of the stations that I like to do with kids—complete with a fifteenth station that includes a bit about the Resurrection. This is kind of like the nineteenth hole back at the golf club; it's not part of the traditional story but it's a great way to end. I like for the kids to walk the Way of the Cross in the context of Easter rather than leaving Jesus in the tomb, and, anyway, it beats showing them Mel Gibson's "The Passion of the Christ."

It was a blustery morning out there, 35 degrees and windy, as Easter fell particularly early that year. In other words, it was perfect Good Friday weather. Who wants 75 degrees and sunny when we're out to mark our Lord's Crucifixion. The boys were great at taking turns reading the stations and then sprinting to the next one. I never realized you could multitask your spiritual life and exercise routine by combining a Good Friday liturgy with wind sprints.

On the way home Ben asked, "Dad, can we do this every year on Good Friday?" Um, I think that could be arranged. I later went to a noonday service by myself at a local church. It was simple, quiet, and contemplative. But the one I most cherished had taken place earlier in the day.

Reflection & Discussion

1 What are your experiences of the liturgies of Holy Week? Do you have any memories of these from your childhood? Can you think of any particularly meaningful spiritual encounters?

2 Have you ever had your feet washed during the Maundy Thursday liturgy? Why or why not? What are some times in your life when you have felt most vulnerable? Where do you find God in such moments?

3 Read the Passion narrative from one of the four gospels (Matthew 26-27; Mark 14-15; Luke 22-23; and John 18-19). What particularly stands out for you this year?

EASTER

Vigil People

"**W**hy is this night different from all other nights?" This question is asked in Jewish homes at the Seder dinner on Passover. It is traditionally asked by the youngest member of the family, or at least the youngest one who can read it out of the Haggadah. It's a leading question, of course, a question that can only be answered in the telling of the story of the faith. And on Passover, that story is the seminal event of the Jewish faith: the story of the exodus out of Egypt.

For Christians, the same question could be asked about Easter eve because the Great Vigil of Easter is also a night different from all other nights—and not just because the clergy get to play with fire.

This night is different from all other nights because it is the night of our own passover. It is the night Jesus Christ passes over from death to life. It is the night that we, as a church, pass over from Lent to Easter;

from darkness to light, from sin to righteousness, and from Crucifixion to Resurrection.

But this passover is not a mere retelling of the story or a recounting of past events. Yes, we remember the events of that first Easter Day, but it doesn't end there. Each year as we gather in vigil, Christ passes over anew. As we gather to tell the stories of our faith from the very beginning of creation, through the rising waters of the flood, the liberating waters of the Red Sea, the sacramental waters of baptism straight through to the empty tomb, Christ passes over anew.

The Easter Vigil truly is a rite of passage but not in the conventional sense. It's not a mere formality, a custom we attend to because tradition so dictates. It's not a rite of passage that keeps us in good social graces with our neighbors, and it's not a coming of age ritual. The Easter Vigil is a rite of passage because it takes us on a journey.

And we all join in this passover journey not as passive observers but as active participants.

The Easter Vigil stands at the heart of who we are and what we do as Christians. It has all the great symbols of our faith: fire, water, light, darkness, bread, wine. And even some lesser-known ones like champagne and jelly beans—at least at my parish since the vigil is always followed up with a champagne and jelly bean reception.

It's true that the Easter Vigil is not everyone's idea of a good time. It's not the best-attended service of the year, and for many people, the thought of either not going to church on Easter Sunday or attending two services within twelve hours is a bewildering concept.

Barbara Harris, the first female bishop in the Anglican Communion, likes to say that as Christians we are an Easter people living in a Good Friday world. I can see that. But if Christians are an Easter people, those who attend the Easter Vigil are a special subset of these people. We are vigil people (not Village People—that's something else). And as vigil people, we gather around the flame, we gather around God's Word, we gather around the baptismal font, and we gather around the altar. This is really what Jesus calls us to do in the first place: to simply gather around him.

If Easter Day is all about Jesus' Resurrection and joy and chocolate bunnies and big hats, the Easter Vigil is literally about the passover. And it's an important piece of the story, a critical piece of the journey from the cross to the empty tomb.

Easter eve is different from all other nights. As
the liturgy proclaims, "For this is the Passover of the
Lord, in which, by hearing his Word and celebrating
his Sacraments, we share in his victory over death"
(*The Book of Common Prayer*, p. 285).

Hunting Season

I like Easter egg hunts, and I play to win. Actually, I haven't been allowed to participate in a hunt for a number of years, which is clearly a form of age discrimination. Just imagine the number of plastic eggs I could amass competing against four- and five-year-olds. I would dominate like LeBron James playing hoops against the junior varsity team.

Most kids can't imagine Easter Day without an Easter egg hunt, and I love the adrenaline-pumping thrill of the hunt. And that was just last year. We hold an annual Easter egg hunt at my parish following Easter services, with the start resembling the Running of the Bulls in Pamplona, Spain. A few parents organize it with help from eager teens who like to hide a few eggs in places no one would ever think to look. That means I occasionally stumble on unfound eggs in mid-August. There's no better reminder of the Resurrection than encountering a gooey, four-month-old melted mixture of chocolate bunny and purple jelly beans inside a plastic egg.

In some religious circles, Easter egg hunts are anathema—something about being pagan in origin. They see the egg as a symbol that predates Christianity. But I like Easter egg hunts and not just because free jelly beans are the best kind. I love watching a young child's face light up with the thrill of discovery. Nothing beats it.

That thrill of discovery was precisely what took place on that first Easter morning. I'm not comparing Christ's Resurrection to an Easter egg hunt, but there is something wonderfully exhilarating about the moment of discovery. The disciples experienced it when they came upon the empty tomb, and children experience it when they find an egg. The hope is

that kids will find that same sense of discovery and excitement as they mature and move more deeply into relationship with God.

I have to admit that my local town's egg hunt, which always takes place on Good Friday, is too much for me. I don't mean to sound crotchety, but an Easter egg hunt on the day we mark Jesus' Crucifixion makes me cringe. Okay, I sound crotchety, but when you're fully immersed in the story of the Passion, there's a great disconnect between these two worlds: life and death, sin and atonement versus the carefree secular egg hunt. There's nothing wrong with the joy associated with this egg-driven game of hide and go seek, but there's a time and a place for it. You can't get to the joy of the Resurrection without first going through the agony of the cross.

My former bishop in Maryland once shared a story about a woman who came to his church just one day a year. She would always come on Good Friday but never at any other time. I remember thinking about how sad that was. Yes, you must go through the haunting despair of the cross in order to comprehend the full joy of the Resurrection but to dwell on the agony of the Crucifixion without ever experiencing Easter is a frightening prospect.

I love the Orthodox approach to Good Friday. It's never viewed as a funeral service for Jesus. That would be inauthentic, because, unlike the first disciples, we know the end of the story. The Orthodox mark the pain of the cross fully in the context of the Resurrection, often setting up a large wooden cross in the middle of the church surrounded by Easter lilies. The contrast between the rough wood of the cross and the lilies, delicate symbols of joy, is a powerful image.

It's an image congruent with the fullness of the gospel message. Out of darkness is light, out of pain is joy, out of death there is life. And, if we can wait until Easter, those jelly beans taste even sweeter. Unless I find them on Labor Day.

The Miraculous Peep

O ne of the great miracles of modern culinary science is the Peep. If you've ever come within arm's length of an Easter basket, you've undoubtedly encountered one. Peeps are those chicken-shaped (and sometimes rabbit-shaped) novelty marshmallow treats that have become forever associated with Easter in America. Ben and Zak, like most kids I know, go nuts for Peeps.

The classic Peep is an amazing shade of yellow; some might call it an unnatural color. I suspect a heavy infusion of the infamous Yellow #5 has something to do with its glow but as far as unnatural goes, the color can't compete with the truly unnatural flavor of a Peep. The combination of artificial dye and a boatload of sugar creates a formidable

Honey, by any chance did you give the boys any of those peeps again?

candy. Think I'm joking? Give your kids four or five Peeps as a bedtime snack and see what happens (although I recommend doing this on a night your spouse is responsible for getting them to bed).

There are some important things to know about the whole Peep phenomenon. Yes, dear reader, I undertook some exhaustive Internet research on your behalf (there are an inconceivable number of websites dedicated to all things Peep). First, though they're only sold at Easter time, Peeps are produced year-round. This is possible because they conveniently have a shelf life of two years. Second, while yellow Peeps are the most popular variety, they also come in lavender, pink, blue, and white. Not exactly liturgical colors but festive nonetheless. Finally, you should know that Peeps never travel alone. They are basically created as Siamese quintuplets, attached at the hip before they're put into packages and shipped to local drugstores.

I'm not exactly sure how the Peep became linked with the marking of our Lord's Crucifixion and Resurrection. The minor miracle of Peep technology pales in comparison. But once we recognize the real miracle of Easter—the empty tomb, Christ's victory over sin and death, and our redemption—we're better attuned to the minor miracles that abound in this life.

In the middle of the spring, it's impossible not to see these minor miracles. I know there's some biological reason why buds turn to flowers—sun, photosynthesis, or whatever. I missed that day in middle school science class. Whatever the scientific reason, these blossoms are also simply a miracle of God's creation. And they're everywhere: in the sunshine, in the distinct smell of spring, and in the first daffodil. The point is that we just need to open our eyes and the miraculous presents itself.

While Peeps might not be the kind of minor miracle we're looking for, reconciling a broken relationship with a friend might be. Or taking the dog for a walk and reveling in the beauty of the spring weather, or walking into a church and recognizing for the first time in awhile that, yes, God loves me unconditionally. The Easter miracle is that God is miraculous, God's creation is miraculous, and we participate and live in the midst of this miracle. We are part of the miracle because we are part of God's creation.

Every year my wife, Bryna, makes a lamb cake for dessert following Easter dinner. She started doing this before we had kids to honor the tradition of her

Polish grandmother. While she's got it down now, the first few years were rough. It didn't help that I mocked her early attempts. The lamb, which was supposed to stand up, invariably keeled over just as she brought it out. It was more like a sacrificial lamb, making it good Easter theology but a lame Easter dessert. One year, after a particularly hideous tumble, I added some red icing to the white frosting to create the Blood of the Lamb. Bryna was not amused.

The lamb cake has become as much a part of our Easter tradition as Peeps. Every time Bryna presents the cake, I'm aware that its upright position is another one of those minor miracles that make life so invigorating.

Now that's what I call a sacrifice.

Parallel Universe

"**A** long time ago, in a galaxy far, far away..." That's not actually how the Easter story begins. On Easter Day we don't dim the lights and watch these iconic words scroll off into the distance on a giant projection screen. You won't find the ushers selling overpriced popcorn and giant boxes of Jujyfruits in the narthex.

But doesn't it sometimes feel that way? That Jesus' life happened a long time ago, in a galaxy far, far away? That somehow when we celebrate Christ's Resurrection, we're marking events that, while familiar, can feel remote or other-worldly? As if the events of that first Easter Day took place in a fantasy world conjured from the imaginations of a trinity of Stephens—Hawking, King, and Spielberg.

Even now, two thousand years later, the Resurrection feels like something that happened in a parallel universe, a place similar to earth but where

A LONG TIME AGO IN A GALAXY FAR AWAY

time is eternal, space is infinite, the laws of physics don't apply, and people wear sandals a lot.

For generations, scientists have explored the notion of a parallel universe. And we've often longed for one, or at least fantasized about the possibilities—it's certainly an enduring theme in science fiction. Maybe the whole idea of a parallel world is about escapism or the hope of a utopian existence or simply the old notion of the (fake Easter) grass always being greener.

But on the surface of things, this whole Resurrection business grates against everything we know to be rational and true: that death is final, that someone doesn't just rise up out of a grave and start walking around.

But that's just the point. Easter flips everything upside-down: our preconceived notions are shattered, the purely rational is transcended, and, yes, we enter a parallel universe where faith collides with conventional wisdom and wins out. Easter draws us into a parallel universe where love conquers all, where death has no dominion over us, where forgiveness wipes away all sin, and where mercy trumps judgment. In this universe, inclusion wins out over exclusion, hope conquers despair, Resurrection and life triumph over Crucifixion and death. That's a place I want to live! The risen Christ invites us all into this parallel universe of Resurrection glory.

In most science fiction, you enter the parallel universe through an elusive secret portal. I'm not a big science fiction guy—I can't even name all the characters in *Star Trek*—but it seems the portal always involves some sort of hidden vortex. The good news for us is that our portal is hardly a secret. Our portal into this parallel universe is the very Easter story we've been proclaiming ever since the women first encountered the empty tomb.

The Easter story, as familiar as it is, still blows the mind, like thinking about infinity or the endless expanse of the universe. In its fullness, the concept of Christ's ultimate sacrifice and Resurrection remains incomprehensible to our limited human minds. But that's the true miracle of Easter, isn't it? God loves us despite our human foibles and weakness and distractedness and myopic views of the world.

The stunning thing about Easter is that this parallel universe isn't mere fantasy or science fiction, and we're not merely witnesses to this miracle of Resurrection but participants in it. Jesus Christ is risen for you and for me. He is risen for the women at the tomb and for the disciples who fled. He is risen to wipe away our individual and collective brokenness. He is risen to offer hope and salvation to a hurting world. He is risen because God's love for us is stronger even than death.

And so, may the joy of this Easter season open up for you an ever-deepening relationship with the God who banishes death and despair and offers us life and hope. And may Christ's victory over the grave draw you into the parallel universe of Resurrection glory.

Reflection & Discussion

1 Have you ever attended the Easter Vigil? If so, what did you find particularly moving?

2 What are some of your family traditions surrounding Easter Day? Do you have a favorite Easter hymn or Easter candy? What is your experience with Easter egg hunts?

3 How have you experienced resurrection in your own life? Has your faith made it easier to mourn the loss of a loved one? How?

Afterword

My favorite church service of the year, by far, is the Easter Vigil. There's fire, darkness, incense, water, and lots of candles as the congregation moves from the darkness of sin and death into the light of Christ. It all adds up to the most dramatic and compelling liturgy on the church calendar.

It is also the service with the greatest room for liturgical error. Jesus will be raised, alleluias will ring out, but at the parishes I've served, I always consider it a successful night if we don't get a visit from the fire department. Priests fumbling around in the dark with fire. What could possibly go wrong?

I've always been fascinated with liturgical bloopers stories from the Easter Vigil. Vestments catching on fire, baptismal fonts being knocked over, flaming pots of incense hitting inert objects. But my favorite story was told to me by the current bishop of the Diocese of Nebraska, J. Scott Barker, when we were both priests in the Diocese of New York.

It took place when Scott was serving as the assistant priest at Trinity Cathedral in Omaha, Nebraska. The cathedral stands across the street from the Omaha Civic Center, and on this Easter weekend, promoters brought in the popular heavy metal rock-and-roll band Guns n' Roses. "All seemed to be well," Scott said, "until that solemn moment when our deacon (a lovely soprano with choir-boy purity of tone) turned on her wireless microphone to get ready to chant the Exsultet. It turns out that the cathedral's wireless was on the same frequency as lead singer Axl Rose's mic, and so instead of the dulcet tones of the beautiful chant, the cathedral congregation heard Axl Rose howling to his fans across the street: 'Welcome to the Jungle!'" And to think, their hit song "Paradise City" would have been so much more liturgically appropriate.

Despite the potential for uninvited liturgical drama, Jesus Christ rises every year. I've found over the years that whatever we do or fail to do, whatever goes right or horribly wrong in liturgy or in life, Jesus' Resurrection always takes place. This is an important reminder that we're not ultimately in control and that our human foibles and machinations serve merely as the backdrop to the Paschal Mystery. I think we can all find great freedom in that.

I hope this book has provided some inspiration as you travel from the wilderness of Lent into the joy of Easter. This time of year gets to the heart of what it means to be a Christian and embracing it is good for the soul.

Oh, and if you've never been to an Easter Vigil, I encourage you to experience one this year. The liturgy, complicated as it may be, is transformative and, especially if your priest catches on fire, it is one you will never forget.

About the author

Tim Schenck is rector of the Episcopal Parish of St. John the Evangelist in Hingham, Massachusetts, on the South Shore of Boston. He is the author of *Dog in the Manger: Finding God in Christmas Chaos,* a companion to *Dust Bunnies in the Basket.* He has also written *What Size Are God's Shoes: Kids, Chaos, and the Spiritual Life* and *Father Tim's Church Survival Guide* (Morehouse). Tim also writes a monthly syndicated column for Gatehouse Media titled "In Good Faith" and blogs at *Clergy Confidential* @www.clergyconfidential.com. When not tending to his parish or drinking single origin coffee, you'll likely find Tim hanging out with his wife, two teenage sons, his dog, and a ferret. Follow him on Twitter @ FatherTim.

About Forward Movement

Forward Movement has been committed to reinvigorating the Church for more than seventy-five years. While we produce great resources like this book, Forward Movement is not a publishing company. We are a ministry. Our mission is to support you in your spiritual journey, to make stronger disciples and followers of Jesus Christ.

Publishing books, daily reflections, small-group studies, and online resources is an important way that we live out this ministry. More than a half million people read our daily devotions through *Forward Day by Day,* which is also available in Spanish and Braille, online and as an app for your smart phones or tablets. It is mailed to more than fifty countries, and we donate nearly 30,000 copies each quarter to prisons, hospitals, and nursing homes. We actively seek partners across the Church and look for ways to provide tools that inspire and challenge.

A ministry of The Episcopal Church, Forward Movement is a nonprofit company completely funded by sales of resources and gifts from generous donors. If you want to learn more about Forward Movement and our resources, please visit us at www.forwardmovement.org.

We are delighted to be doing this work and invite your prayers and support.